FAVORITE BIBLE STORIES

Activity Book

Favorite Bible Stories Activity Book

Copyright © 2019. All rights reserved

This Activity Book may not be reproduced in whole or in part in any manner without written permission from Bible Pathway Adventures.

ISBN: 978-1-98-858540-6

Author: Pip Reid
Illustrator: Thomas Barnett
Creative Director: Curtis Reid

For free Bible resources and Teacher Packs including coloring pages, worksheets, quizzes and more visit our website at:

www.biblepathwayadventures.com

◈ INTRODUCTION ◈

Enjoy teaching your children about the Bible with Bible Pathway Adventures' Favorite Bible Stories Activity Book. From Adam and Eve to Paul's shipwreck, your children will love learning about the Bible's most famous characters in this fun and engaging way.

Each coloring worksheet includes scripture references for further Bible reading, and a handy answer key for educators and parents. The perfect discipleship resource for Homeschoolers, Sabbath and Sunday School teachers, and families.

Bible Pathway Adventures helps teachers and parents teach children a Biblical faith in a fun creative way. We do this via our illustrated storybooks, Teacher Packs, and printable activities – all available on our website: www.biblepathwayadventures.com

The search for Truth is more fun than Tradition!

◆◇ TABLE OF CONTENTS ◇◆

Introduction 3
Take a trip back in time 7

Adam & Eve 8
Cain & Abel 9
Noah 10
Abraham 11
Lot's Escape 12
Isaac & Rebekah 13
Jacob & Esau 14
Rachel 15
Joseph 16
Moses 17
Pharaoh 18
Miriam 19
Aaron 20
Caleb 21
Joshua 22
Rahab 23
Balaam 24
Gideon 25
Ruth & Boaz 26
Deborah 27
Samson & Delilah 28
Hannah 29
Samuel 30

King Saul	31
David & Goliath	32
Jonathan	33
Benaiah	34
David & Bathsheba	35
Solomon	36
Jezebel	37
Queen of Sheba	38
Amos	39
Isaiah	40
Elijah	41
Elisha	42
Daniel	43
Mordecai	44
Esther	45
Queen Vashti	46
Nehemiah	47
Jonah	48
Job	49
John the Baptist	50
Elizabeth	51
Mary & Joseph	52
Birth of Yeshua	53
Crucifixion	54
Resurrection	55
The Good Samaritan	56
Wedding at Cana	57
Loaves and Fishes	58
Calming the Storm	59
Prodigal Son	60
Wise & Foolish Virgins	61

The Lost Sheep	62
The Sower	63
The Magi	64
Peter & Cornelius	65
Judas	66
Mary Magdalene	67
Raising of Lazarus	68
Stoning of Stephen	69
Road to Damascus	70
Shipwrecked!	71
Priscilla & Aquila	72
Tabitha, Arise!	73
Philip & the Ethiopian	74
Timothy	75
Mary & Martha	76
Zacchaeus	77
Answer Key	78
Discover more Activity Books!	82

◇◆ TAKE A TRIP BACK IN TIME ◆◇

Our vision is to provide culturally, historically, and biblically sound materials to help you teach your children a Biblical faith. When we read the Bible in the context of the ancient Hebrew culture, it comes alive and unlocks the beauty and richness of the faith.

Why do we use Hebrew names like Yeshua? Or sometimes include the Hebrew names for God like Yah? Because understanding these ancient names and cultures helps us unlock the richness of each Biblical account – a richness and understanding that can get lost, changed, or watered-down when only seen from a modern Western perspective.

For example, Matthew 26:34 says… "Before the rooster crows, you will deny me three times." In its cultural and historical context, this was not actually a rooster crowing but the Temple Crier, a priest who announced the morning Temple services and sacrifices at the time of Yeshua. Did you know the modern English name of 'Jesus' has only been used for 500 years? This means Mary and the disciples would have called the Messiah by His actual Hebrew name, Yeshua or Yehoshua, which means, 'God saves,' or 'God is my salvation.' Isn't that wonderful!

So…let's take a trip back in time and enjoy the richness of the Bible!

Adam & Eve

Read Genesis 2:8 and write the Bible verse below.

....

....

....

1. Where did God plant a garden?

....

....

2. Who named all the birds and animals?

....

....

3. What did the serpent say to Eve?

....

....

Draw your favorite scene from this story.

What could the life of Adam & Eve teach me?

....

....

God used Adam & Eve to...

....

....

Cain & Abel

Read Genesis 4:9 and write the Bible verse below.

....

....

....

1. What did Cain offer for a sacrifice?
....
....

2. What did Cain do to Abel?
....
....

3. After Cain fled from God, where did he live?
....
....

Draw your favorite scene from this story.

What could the life of Cain & Abel teach me?	God used Cain & Abel to...
....	....

Noah

Read Genesis 6:17 and write the Bible verse below.

....

....

....

1. How long was Noah's Ark?

....

....

2. How many pairs of 'clean' animals did Noah take on the Ark?

....

....

3. For how many days did rain fall on the earth?

....

....

Draw your favorite scene from this story.

What could the life of Noah teach me?	God used Noah to...
....	....
....	....

Abraham

Read Genesis 15:5 and write the Bible verse below.

....

....

....

1. Who was Abraham's wife?
....
....

2. Where did Abraham go to escape the famine?
....
....

3. What did God promise Abraham in Genesis 15:4?
....
....

Draw your favorite scene from this story.

What could the life of Abraham teach me?	God used Abraham to…
....	....

Lot's escape

Read Genesis 19:24 and write the Bible verse below.

....

....

....

1. How many angels visited Sodom?
....
....

2. What fell on Sodom and Gomorrah?
....
....

3. What happened to Lot's wife when she looked back?
....
....

Draw your favorite scene from this story.

What could the life of Lot teach me?	God used Lot to...
....	....

Isaac & Rebekah

Read Genesis 24:67 and write the Bible verse below.

....

....

....

1. Where did Abraham's servant go to find a wife for Isaac?

....

....

2. Where did the servant find Rebekah?

....

....

3. What jewelry did the servant give Rebekah?

....

....

Draw your favorite scene from this story.

What could the life of Isaac and Rebekah teach me?	God used Isaac and Rebekah to...
....	....
....	....

www.biblepathwayadventures.com
Favorite Bible Stories Activity Book

Jacob & Esau

Read Genesis 25:34 and write the Bible verse below.

....

....

....

1. Who was Jacob and Esau's father?

....

....

2. How did God describe Esau?

....

....

3. For what food did Esau sell his birthright?

....

....

Draw your favorite scene from this story.

What could the life of Jacob & Esau teach me?	God used Jacob & Esau to...
....	....
....	....

Rachel

Read Genesis 29:18 and write the Bible verse below.

....

....

....

1. How many years did Jacob agree to work for Rachel?

....

....

2. Who were Rachel's two sons?

....

....

3. What did Rachel steal from her father's tent?

....

....

Draw your favorite scene from this story.

What could the life of Rachel teach me?	God used Rachel to...
....	....
....	....

Joseph

Read Genesis 37:3 and write the Bible verse below.

....

....

....

1. What gift did Jacob give Joseph?

....
....

2. What was Joseph's first dream?

....
....

3. How did Joseph's brothers get rid of him?

....
....

Draw your favorite scene from this story.

What could the life of Joseph teach me?	God used Joseph to...

Moses

Read Exodus 3:10 and write the Bible verse below.

....

....

....

1. How did God appear to Moses in the desert?

....

....

2. Who did Moses ask to free the Hebrews?

....

....

3. Who stood with Moses before Pharaoh?

....

....

Draw your favorite scene from this story.

What could the life of Moses teach me?	God used Moses to...
....	....
....	....

Pharaoh

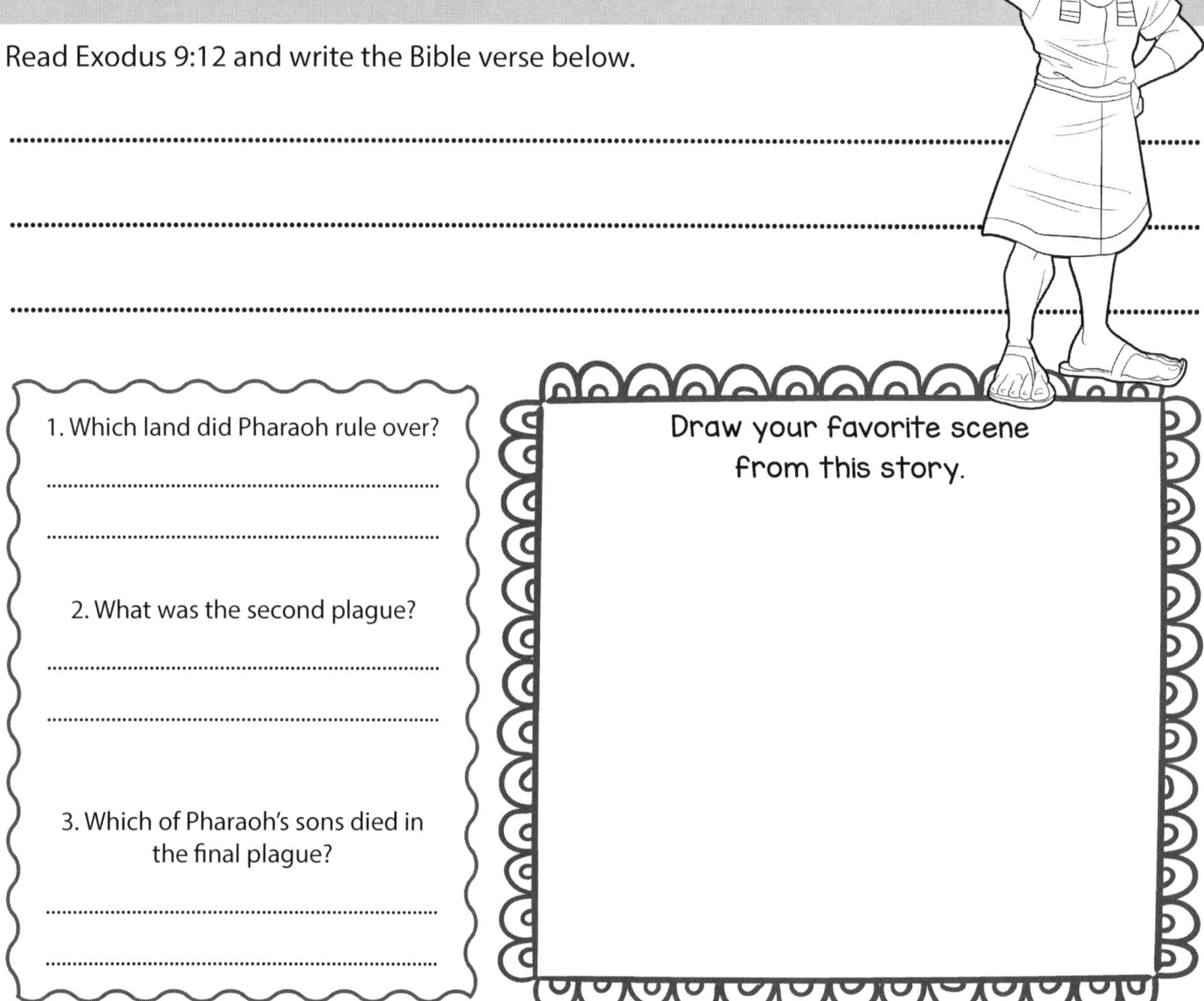

Read Exodus 9:12 and write the Bible verse below.

....

....

....

1. Which land did Pharaoh rule over?

....

....

2. What was the second plague?

....

....

3. Which of Pharaoh's sons died in the final plague?

....

....

Draw your favorite scene from this story.

What could the life of Pharaoh teach me?	God used Pharaoh to...
....	....

Miriam

Read Exodus 2:4 and write the Bible verse below.

....

....

....

1. Who were Miriam's two brothers?
....
....

2. Why did Miriam wait in the reeds by the river?
....
....

3. Who did Miriam fetch to take care of the baby Moses?
....
....

Draw your favorite scene from this story.

What could the life of Miriam teach me?	God used Miriam to...

Aaron

Read Exodus 32:24 and write the Bible verse below.

....

....

....

1. Who did the Israelites ask to make a calf?

....

....

2. What metal was the calf made from?

....

....

3. How did Moses destroy the calf?

....

....

Draw your favorite scene from this story.

What could the life of Aaron teach me?	God used Aaron to...
....	....
....	....

Caleb

Read Numbers 13:30 and write the Bible verse below.

....

....

....

1. Who was Caleb's father?

....

....

2. How many spies did Moses send into Canaan?

....

....

3. How long did Caleb and the spies explore Canaan?

....

....

Draw your favorite scene from this story.

What could the life of Caleb teach me?

....

....

God used Caleb to...

....

....

Joshua

Read Joshua 3:7 and write the Bible verse below.

....

....

....

1. Which river did the Israelites cross to enter Canaan?
   ....
   ....

2. Who carried the Ark across the river?
   ....
   ....

3. What did Joshua do after the Israelites crossed the river?
   ....
   ....

Draw your favorite scene from this story.

What could the life of Joshua teach me?	God used Joshua to...

Rahab

Read Joshua 2:15 and write the Bible verse below.

....

....

....

1. Where in Jericho was Rahab's house?
....
....

2. How did Rahab hide the spies?
....
....

3. How did Rahab help the spies escape?
....
....

Draw your favorite scene from this story.

What could the life of Rahab teach me?	God used Rahab to...
....	....
....	....

Balaam

Read Numbers 22:35 and write the Bible verse below.

....

....

....

1. What animal spoke to Balaam?
....
....

2. What did Balaam do after the Angel spared his life?
....
....

3. How many times did Balaam bless the Israelites?
....
....

Draw your favorite scene from this story.

What could the life of Balaam teach me?	God used Balaam to...
....	....
....	....

Bible Pathway Adventures

Gideon

Read Judges 6:34 and write the Bible verse below.

....

....

....

1. What Midianite altar did Gideon destroy?

....

....

2. What did Gideon do to receive a sign from God?

....

....

3. What did Gideon use to defeat the Midianites?

....

....

Draw your favorite scene from this story.

What could the life of Gideon teach me?	God used Gideon to...
....	....
....	....

www.biblepathwayadventures.com
Favorite Bible Stories Activity Book

© BPA Publishing Ltd 2019

Ruth & Boaz

Read Ruth 1:16 and write the Bible verse below.

....

....

....

1. Where did Ruth and Boaz first meet?
....
....

2. What did Boaz offer Ruth to eat?
....
....

3. On the threshing floor, where did Ruth sleep?
....
....

Draw your favorite scene from this story.

What could the life of Ruth & Boaz teach me?	God used Ruth & Boaz to...
....	....
....	....

Deborah

Read Judges 4:4 and write the Bible verse below.

....

....

....

1. What were Deborah's two roles?
....
....

2. Where did Deborah sit to give judgment?
....
....

3. How many men fought the Canaanites?
....
....

Draw your favorite scene from this story.

What could the life of Deborah teach me?	God used Deborah to...

Samson & Delilah

Read Judges 16:6 and write the Bible verse below.

....

....

....

1. Where did Delilah live?
....
....

2. What did Delilah use to first bind Samson?
....
....

3. What was the secret of Samson's strength?
....
....

Draw your favorite scene from this story.

What could the life of Samson teach me?	God used Samson to…
....	....
....	....

Hannah

Read 1 Samuel 1:20 and write the Bible verse below.

....

....

....

1. Why did Hannah cry at the temple?

....

....

2. What name did Hannah give her son?

....

....

3. What did Hannah bring her son each year?

....

....

Draw your favorite scene from this story.

What could the life of Hannah teach me?	God used Hannah to...
....	....

Samuel

Read 1 Samuel 10:24 and write the Bible verse below.

....

....

....

1. What did the Israelites demand from Samuel?

....

....

2. What did Samuel warn them a king would do?

....

....

3. Who was the first king of Israel?

....

....

Draw your favorite scene from this story.

What could the life of Samuel teach me?	God used Samuel to...
....	....
....	....

King Saul

Read 1 Samuel 9:16 and write the Bible verse below.

....

....

....

1. Saul was of which tribe of Israel?
....
....

2. Which enemies did Saul fight many times?
....
....

3. Which prophet anointed Saul as king?
....
....

Draw your favorite scene from this story.

What could the life of Saul teach me?

God used Saul to...

David & Goliath

Read 1 Samuel 17:45 and write the Bible verse below.

....

....

....

1. How tall was Goliath?
....
....

2. How many stones did David pick out of the stream?
....
....

3. How did David kill Goliath?
....
....

Draw your favorite scene from this story.

What could the life of David teach me?
....
....

God used David to...
....
....

Jonathan

Read 1 Samuel 20:33 and write the Bible verse below.

....
....
....

1. Who was Jonathan's father?
....
....

2. With whom did Jonathan make a covenant?
....
....

3. Why did Saul throw a spear at Jonathan?
....
....

Draw your favorite scene from this story.

What could the life of Jonathan teach me?	God used Jonathan to...
....	....
....	....

Benaiah

Read 2 Samuel 23:20 and write the Bible verse below.

....

....

....

1. Benaiah was in charge of which king's bodyguard?

....

....

2. What animal did Benaiah kill on a snowy day?

....

....

3. Who was Benaiah's father?

....

....

Draw your favorite scene from this story.

What could the life of Benaiah teach me?	God used Benaiah to...

David & Bathsheba

Read 2 Samuel 11:3 and write the Bible verse below.

....

....

....

1. What was Bathsheba doing when David saw her?

....
....

2. Who did David have killed in battle?

....
....

3. What did Bathsheba do when she heard Uriah was dead?

....
....

Draw your favorite scene from this story.

What could the life of Bathsheba teach me?	God used Bathsheba to...
....	....
....	....

Solomon

Read 1 Kings 3:12 and write the Bible verse below.

....

....

....

1. How did Solomon show that he loved God?

....

....

2. What gift did God give Solomon?

....

....

3. What did God promise Solomon if he obeyed His instructions?

....

....

Draw your favorite scene from this story.

What could the life of Solomon teach me?	God used Solomon to...
....	....
....	....

Jezebel

Read 1 Kings 21:7 and write the Bible verse below.

....

....

....

1. Who was Jezebel's husband?
....
....

2. What did Jezebel do to Naboth?
....
....

3. Why did Elijah escape to Beersheba?
....
....

Draw your favorite scene from this story.

What could the life of Jezebel teach me?	God used Jezebel to...
....	....
....	....

Queen of Sheba

Read 1 Kings 10:1 and write the Bible verse below.

....

....

....

1. Why did the Queen of Sheba visit Solomon?

....

....

2. What gifts did the queen bring with her?

....

....

3. What gifts did Solomon give the queen?

....

....

Draw your favorite scene from this story.

What could the life of the Queen of Sheba teach me?	God used the Queen of Sheba to...
....	....
....	....

Amos

Read Amos 7:15 and write the Bible verse below.

....

....

....

1. What was Amos' job?

....

....

2. Where was Amos from?

....

....

3. Who does Amos say will go into captivity?

....

....

Draw your favorite scene from this story.

What could the life of Amos teach me?	God used Amos to...
....	....
....	....

Isaiah

Read 2 Kings 20:1 and write the Bible verse below.

....

....

....

1. What was Isaiah's job?

....

....

2. Who was Isaiah's father?

....

....

3. What did Isaiah tell King Hezekiah while he was sick?

....

....

Draw your favorite scene from this story.

What could the life of Isaiah teach me?	God used Isaiah to...
....	....

Elijah

Read 1 Kings 18:38 and write the Bible verse below.

....

....

....

1. Where did Elijah meet the false prophets?

....

....

2. What animal did Elijah sacrifice?

....

....

3. What did the fire of God burn up?

....

....

Draw your favorite scene from this story.

What could the life of Elijah teach me?

....

....

God used Elijah to...

....

....

Elisha

Read 2 Kings 2:2 and write the Bible verse below.

....

....

....

1. What separated Elisha and Elijah?
....
....

2. How did Elijah go up to Heaven?
....
....

3. What did Elisha do with Elijah's garment?
....
....

Draw your favorite scene from this story.

What could the life of Elisha teach me?	God used Elisha to...
....	....

Daniel

Read Daniel 6:22 and write the Bible verse below.

....

....

....

1. Who plotted to kill Daniel?

....

....

2. Why was Daniel thrown to the lions?

....

....

3. Who protected Daniel from the lions?

....

....

Draw your favorite scene from this story.

What could the life of Daniel teach me?	God used Daniel to...

Mordecai

Read Esther 8:15 and write the Bible verse below.

....

....

....

1. Which girl did Mordecai help raise?
....
....

2. What instructions did Mordecai give Esther?
....
....
....

3. How did the King honor Mordecai for saving his life?
....
....
....

Draw your favorite scene from this story.

What could the life of Mordecai teach me?	God used Mordecai to...

Esther

Read Esther 4:14 and write the Bible verse below.

....

....

....

1. What did the king do when Esther came before him uninvited?
....
....

2. Who did Esther invite to her banquets?
....
....

3. How did the king stop the destruction of the Hebrews?
....
....

Draw your favorite scene from this story.

What could the life of Esther teach me?	God used Esther to...

Queen Vashti

Read Esther 1:9 and write the Bible verse below.

....

....

....

1. Who was Queen Vashti's husband?
....
....

2. Why did the king want to show Vashti to the people?
....
....

3. Did Vashti obey her husband?
....
....

Draw your favorite scene from this story.

What could the life of Vashti teach me?	God used Vashti to...
....	....
....	....

Nehemiah

Read Nehemiah 2:5 and write the Bible verse below.

....

....

....

1. What was Nehemiah's job?

....

....

2. What did Nehemiah ask the king of Persia?

....

....

3. What did Nehemiah do when he reached Jerusalem?

....

....

Draw your favorite scene from this story.

What could the life of Nehemiah teach me?	God used Nehemiah to...
....	....
....	....

Jonah

Read Jonah 1:17 and write the Bible verse below.

....

....

....

1. Where did God send Jonah?
....
....

2. How long was Jonah inside the fish?
....
....

3. What did Jonah do when he reached Nineveh?
....
....

Draw your favorite scene from this story.

What could the life of Jonah teach me?	God used Jonah to...
....	....
....	....

Job

Read Job 1:1 and write the Bible verse below.

....

....

....

1. Where did Job and his family live?

....

....

2. Before his trials, how many children did Job have?

....

....

3. How did Job's children die?

....

....

Draw your favorite scene from this story.

What could the life of Job teach me?

....

....

God used Job to...

....

....

John the Baptist

Read Matthew 3:1 and write the Bible verse below.

....

....

....

1. What type of insect did John like to eat?

....

....

2. In which river did John baptize people?

....

....

3. Who baptized Yeshua?

....

....

Draw your favorite scene from this story.

What could the life of John the Baptist teach me?

....

....

God used John the Baptist to...

....

....

Elizabeth

Read Luke 1:80 and write the Bible verse below.

....

....

....

1. Why did Elizabeth have no children?
....
....

2. What did the angel say to Zechariah?
....
....

3. What was the name of Elizabeth's son?
....
....

Draw your favorite scene from this story.

What could the life of Elizabeth teach me?	God used Elizabeth to...
....	....
....	....

www.biblepathwayadventures.com
Favorite Bible Stories Activity Book

Mary & Joseph

Read Matthew 2:13 and write the Bible verse below.

....

....

....

1. In which village did Mary & Joseph live?

....

....

2. Why did Mary & Joseph travel to Bethlehem?

....

....

3. To which country did Mary, Joseph, and Yeshua escape?

....

....

Draw your favorite scene from this story.

What could the life of Mary & Joseph teach me?	God used Mary & Joseph to...
....	....
....	....

www.biblepathwayadventures.com
Favorite Bible Stories Activity Book

© BPA Publishing Ltd 2019

Birth of Yeshua

Read Matthew 1:21 and write the Bible verse below.

....

....

....

1. Where was Yeshua born?
....
....

2. Who was king of Judea at this time?
....
....

3. How many Magi visited Yeshua?
....
....

Draw your favorite scene from this story.

What could the life of Yeshua teach me?

God used Yeshua to…

Crucifixion

Read Matthew 27:50 and write the Bible verse below.

....

....

....

1. Who sentenced Yeshua to die?
....
....

2. Where was Yeshua crucified?
....
....

3. Who was crucified next to Yeshua?
....
....

Draw your favorite scene from this story.

What could Yeshua's death teach me?	God used Yeshua's death to...
....	....

Resurrection

Read Matthew 28:6 and write the Bible verse below.

....

....

....

1. Yeshua rose from the grave on which Feast?

....

....

2. Who met Yeshua outside the tomb?

....

....

3. Which disciple doubted Yeshua was alive?

....

....

Draw your favorite scene from this story.

What could Yeshua's resurrection teach me?	God used Yeshua's resurrection to...
....	....
....	....

The Good Samaritan

Read Luke 10:34 and write the Bible verse below.

....

....

....

1. Where was the traveler going?
....
....

2. What happened to the traveler on this road?
....
....

3. What did the Samaritan do to help the traveler?
....
....

Draw your favorite scene from this story.

What could this parable teach me?	Yeshua used this parable to...
....	....
....	....

Wedding at Cana

Read John 2:11 and write the Bible verse below.

....

....

....

1. Who was invited to a wedding?
....
....

2. What did Yeshua say to the servants?
....
....

3. What did Yeshua turn water into?
....
....

Draw your favorite scene from this story.

What could this miracle teach me?	Yeshua used this miracle to…
....	....
....	....

www.biblepathwayadventures.com
Favorite Bible Stories Activity Book

© BPA Publishing Ltd 2019

Loaves and Fishes

Read John 6:9 and write the Bible verse below.

....

....

....

1. How many men gathered to hear Yeshua teach?

....

....

2. What did Yeshua do when He held the bread?

....

....

3. How many baskets were filled with leftovers?

....

....

Draw your favorite scene from this story.

What could this miracle teach me?	Yeshua used this miracle to...
....	....
....	....

www.biblepathwayadventures.com
Favorite Bible Stories Activity Book

© BPA Publishing Ltd 2019

Calming the Storm

Read Mark 4:41 and write the Bible verse below.

....

....

....

1. What happened on the sea of Galilee?
....
....

2. What did the disciples say to Yeshua when they woke Him?
....
....

3. How did Yeshua calm the storm?
....
....

Draw your favorite scene from this story.

What could this miracle teach me?	Yeshua used this miracle to...
....	....

Prodigal Son

Read Luke 15:32 and write the Bible verse below.

....

....

....

1. Which son asked for his inheritance?
....
....

2. After this son wasted his money, what job did he get?
....
....

3. How did the father celebrate his son's return?
....
....

Draw your favorite scene from this story.

What could this parable teach me?	Yeshua used this parable to…
....	....
....	....

www.biblepathwayadventures.com
Favorite Bible Stories Activity Book

Wise & Foolish Virgins

Read Matthew 25:1 and write the Bible verse below.

....

....

....

1. How many virgins were wise?

   ....

   ....

2. What did the foolish virgins ask the wise virgins?

   ....

   ....

3. What happened while the foolish virgins went to buy oil?

   ....

   ....

Draw your favorite scene from this story.

What could this parable teach me?	Yeshua used this parable to...
....	....
....	....

The Lost Sheep

Read Matthew 18:14 and write the Bible verse below.

....

....

....

1. How many sheep did the man have?
....
....

2. Where did he leave the ninety-nine sheep?
....
....

3. What did the man do when he found the missing sheep?
....
....

Draw your favorite scene from this story.

What could this parable teach me?	Yeshua used this parable to…
....	....
....	....

The Sower

Read Mark 4:3 and write the Bible verse below.

....

....

....

1. What happened to seeds that fell among thorns?

....

....

2. What happened to seeds that fell into good soil?

....

....

3. What happens to people who hear the Word and accept it?

....

....

Draw your favorite scene from this story.

What could this parable teach me?	Yeshua used this parable to…
....	....
....	....

The Magi

Read Matthew 2:10 and write the Bible verse below.

....

....

....

1. How did the Magi know Yeshua had been born?

....

....

2. What did the Magi do when they saw Yeshua?

....

....

3. What gifts did the Magi give Yeshua?

....

....

Draw your favorite scene from this story.

What could the story of the Magi teach me?	God used the Magi to...
....	....

Peter & Cornelius

Read Acts 10:44 and write the Bible verse below.

....

....

....

1. What was Cornelius' job?
....
....

2. What instruction was Cornelius given in a vision?
....
....

3. What did Peter command Cornelius and his family to do?
....
....

Draw your favorite scene from this story.

What could the story of Peter & Cornelius teach me?	God used Peter to...
....	....

Judas

Read Luke 22:48 and write the Bible verse below.

....

....

....

1. Who paid Judas to betray Yeshua?
....
....

2. How much money was Judas given to betray Yeshua?
....
....

3. Where did Judas betray Yeshua?
....
....

Draw your favorite scene from this story.

What could the life of Judas teach me?

....

God used Judas to...

....

Mary Magdalene

Read John 20:18 and write the Bible verse below.

....

....

....

1. Who told Mary that Yeshua had risen?
   ....
   ....

2. Who did Yeshua first appear to after His resurrection?
   ....
   ....

3. What did Mary tell the disciples after she had seen Yeshua?
   ....
   ....

Draw your favorite scene from this story.

What could the life of Mary Magdalene teach me?	God used Mary Magdalene to...
....	....
....	....

Lazarus

Read John 11:11 and write the Bible verse below.

....

....

....

1. Who were Lazarus' two sisters?
....
....

2. What type of tomb was Lazarus' body placed inside?
....
....

3. What did Yeshua say to Lazarus while he was in the tomb?
....
....

Draw your favorite scene from this story.

What could this miracle teach me?	Yeshua used this miracle to…
....	....
....	....

Stephen

Read Acts 6:15 and write the Bible verse below.

....

....

....

1. Who was Stephen accused of speaking against?
....
....

2. Who looked after the coats while Stephen was stoned?
....
....

3. Where did the stoning of Stephen take place?
....
....

Draw your favorite scene from this story.

What could the life of Stephen teach me?
....
....

God used Stephen to…
....
....

Road to Damascus

Read Acts 9:8 and write the Bible verse below.

....

....

....

1. Why did Saul travel to Damascus?

....

....

2. Who gave Saul letters to the synagogues in Damascus?

....

....

3. Who spoke to Saul on the road to Damascus?

....

....

Draw your favorite scene from this story.

What could the life of Saul teach me?	God used Saul to...
....	....
....	....

Shipwrecked!

Read Acts 28:1 and write the Bible verse below.

....

....

....

1. Why did Paul not want to sail past Yom Kippur?

....

....

2. On which island was Paul shipwrecked?

....

....

3. What came out of the fire and attacked Paul?

....

....

Draw your favorite scene from this story.

What could the life of Paul teach me?

....

....

God used Paul to...

....

....

Priscilla & Aquila

Read Acts 18:2 and write the Bible verse below.

....

....

....

1. What was Priscilla and Aquila's profession?

....

....

2. Why did they leave Italy and go to Corinth?

....

....

3. In which city did Paul stay with Priscilla and Aquila?

....

....

Draw your favorite scene from this story.

What could the life of Priscilla & Aquila teach me?	God used Priscilla & Aquila to...
....	....
....	....

Tabitha, Arise!

Read Acts 9:36 and write the Bible verse below.

....
....
....

1. Why did Tabitha die?
....
....

2. How many men went to fetch Peter?
....
....

3. What happened after Peter spoke to Tabitha?
....
....

Draw your favorite scene from this story.

What could this miracle teach me?
....
....

God used this miracle to…
....
....

Favorite Bible Stories Activity Book

Philip & the Ethiopian

Read Acts 8:26 and write the Bible verse below.

....

....

....

1. Who did Philip meet on the road to Gaza?

....

....

2. What scriptures was the Ethiopian reading?

....

....

3. Who did Philip explain the scriptures were about?

....

....

Draw your favorite scene from this story.

What could the life of Philip teach me?	God used Philip to...
....	....
....	....

Timothy

Read Acts 16:1 and write the Bible verse below.

....

....

....

1. Where did Paul and Timothy first meet?

....

....

2. What nationality was Timothy's father?

....

....

3. Through which two regions did Paul and Timothy travel?

....

....

Draw your favorite scene from this story.

What could the life of Timothy teach me?	God used Timothy to...

Mary & Martha

Read John 12:1 and write the Bible verse below.

....

....

....

1. Where did Mary and Martha live?
....
....

2. Who anointed Yeshua with perfume?
....
....

3. What type of perfume was used to anoint Yeshua?
....
....

Draw your favorite scene from this story.

What could the life of Mary & Martha teach me?	God used Mary & Martha to…
....	....
....	....

Zacchaeus

Read Luke 19:5 and write the Bible verse below.

....

....

....

1. What was Zacchaeus' job?
....
....

2. Why did Zacchaeus climb a tree?
....
....

3. How much of his goods did Zacchaeus promise the poor?
....
....

Draw your favorite scene from this story.

What could the life of Zacchaeus teach me?

God used Zacchaeus to...

ANSWER KEY

Adam & Eve
1. Eden
2. Adam
3. "You will not surely die."

Cain & Abel
1. Fruit & vegetables
2. Killed him
3. Land of Nod, east of Eden

Noah
1. 300 cubits
2. Seven pairs
3. Forty days

Abraham
1. Sarah
2. Land of Egypt
3. A son (heir)

Lot's Escape
1. Two angels
2. Fire and sulfur (brimstone) out of heaven
3. She turned into a pillar of salt

Isaac & Rebekah
1. Mesopotamia
2. By a spring
3. A gold ring and two bracelets

Jacob & Esau
1. Isaac
2. A skillful hunter and a man of the field
3. Bowl of lentil stew and some bread

Rachel
1. Seven years
2. Benjamin and Joseph
3. Household idols

Joseph
1. A long-sleeved robe
2. Bundles of wheat bowing down to other bundles
3. Threw him in a pit and sold him to strangers

Moses
1. In a burning bush
2. Pharaoh
3. Aaron

Pharaoh
1. Land of Egypt
2. Plague of frogs
3. Pharaoh's firstborn son

Miriam
1. Moses and Aaron
2. To see what would happen to baby Moses
3. Her mother

Aaron
1. Aaron
2. Gold
3. Melted it in the fire and ground it to fine dust

Caleb
1. Jephunneh
2. Twelve spies
3. Forty days

Joshua
1. Jordan River
2. The priests
3. Set up twelve stones, one for each of the tribes of Israel

Rahab
1. In the city wall
2. Under flax on the roof of her house
3. Used a rope to help the men escape through a window

Balaam
1. A donkey
2. Traveled to Moab to meet King Balak
3. Three times

Gideon
1. Altar of Baal
2. Put a fleece on the ground
3. Shofars and jars with torches inside

Ruth & Boaz
1. Boaz's field
2. Bread and roasted grain
3. At Boaz's feet

Deborah
1. Prophetess and judge
2. Under a palm tree between Ramah and Bethel
3. Ten thousand (from the tribes of Naphtali and Zebulon)

Samson & Delilah
1. Valley of Sorek
2. Seven fresh bowstrings
3. His hair

Hannah
1. Because she could not have children
2. Samuel
3. A robe

Samuel
1. A king
2. Make them servants, tax them, and take their sons to be soldiers
3. Saul

King Saul
1. Benjamin
2. The Philistines
3. Samuel

David & Goliath
1. About 9 feet 9 inches
2. Five stones
3. David hit Goliath with a stone from his sling, and then chopped off his head

Jonathan
1. King Saul
2. David
3. Because Jonathan protected David from Saul

Benaiah
1. King David
2. A lion
3. Jehoida

David & Bathsheba
1. Bathing
2. Uriah
3. Bathsheba mourned his death

Solomon
1. He obeyed God's instructions
2. Wisdom
3. A long life

Jezebel
1. Ahab
2. Had Naboth killed so Ahab could possess his vineyard
3. To escape from Jezebel

Queen of Sheba
1. To test Solomon with difficult questions
2. Camels carrying spices, gold and precious stones
3. Everything she desired

Amos
1. Prophet / shepherd / gatherer of sycamore fruit (Amos 7)
2. Tekoa
3. The people of Syria

Isaiah
1. Prophet
2. Amos
3. God will heal you, you will live another 15 years, and God will deliver you and the city from the Assyrians

Elijah
1. Mount Carmel
2. Bull
3. Water, stones, soil and sacrifice

Elisha
1. A chariot of fire and horses of fire
2. In a whirlwind
3. Struck the water and it divided into two

Daniel
1. A group of Magi
2. For praying to Yahweh, the god of Abraham, Isaac and Jacob
3. An angel of God

Mordecai
1. Esther
2. "Do not tell anyone you are a Hebrew, or who I am."
3. Mordecai was led on horseback through the city

Esther
1. Held out his golden scepter
2. The king & Haman
3. Sent letters throughout Persia allowing the Hebrews to defend themselves

Queen Vashti
1. King Ahasuerus
2. She was beautiful
3. No - Vashti refused to go and meet her husband

Nehemiah
1. Cup-bearer to the king of Persia
2. For permission to return to Jerusalem and rebuild the city walls
3. Inspected the city walls

Jonah
1. The city of Nineveh
2. Three days and three nights
3. Told the people to repent

Job
1. Uz
2. Ten children (seven sons, three daughters)
3. A house fell on them

John the Baptist
1. Locusts
2. Jordan River
3. John the Baptist

Elizabeth
1. She was barren
2. You will have a son and you will name him John
3. John

Mary & Joseph
1. Nazareth
2. For the census
3. Land of Egypt

Birth of Yeshua
1. Bethlehem
2. King Herod
3. The Bible doesn't say

Crucifixion
1. Pilate, the Roman governor
2. Golgotha
3. Two criminals

Resurrection
1. Feast of First Fruits
2. Mary Magdalene
3. Thomas

The Good Samaritan
1. Jericho
2. He was robbed and beaten
3. Cleaned the traveler's wounds and paid an innkeeper to take care of him

Wedding at Cana
1. Yeshua, His mother, and His disciples
2. "Fill the jars with water."
3. Wine

Loaves and Fishes
1. 5000 men
2. He blessed the bread
3. Twelve baskets

Calming the Storm
1. A windstorm began
2. "Teacher, do you not care that we are perishing?"
3. He rebuked the wind and said to the sea, "Peace! Be still!"

Prodigal Son
1. Youngest son
2. Feeding pigs
3. Killed a fatted calf and had a party

Wise & Foolish Virgins
1. Five virgins
2. Give us some of your oil for our lamps are going out
3. The bridegroom arrived and went into the wedding with the wise virgins, and shut the door

The Lost Sheep
1. 100 sheep
2. On the mountains
3. He rejoiced

The Sower
1. The thorns grew up and choked the seed, and no grain grew
2. The seeds produced grain, growing up and increasing and yielding thirtyfold, sixtyfold and a hundredfold
3. They produce good fruit, thirtyfold, sixtyfold, and a hundredfold

The Magi
1. They saw a bright star in the sky
2. Bowed down and worshipped Him
3. Gold, frankincense and myrrh

Peter & Cornelius
1. Roman centurion
2. Send men to Joppa and fetch Peter
3. Be baptized (immersed) in the name of Yeshua the Messiah

Judas
1. The religious leaders (priests)
2. Thirty pieces of silver
3. Garden of Gethsemane

Mary Magdalene
1. An angel
2. Mary Magdalene
3. "I have seen Yeshua!"

Lazarus
1. Mary and Martha
2. A cave with a stone door
3. "Lazarus, come out."

Stephen
1. Moses, the Torah, and God
2. Paul
3. Outside Jerusalem

Road to Damascus
1. To find and arrest disciples of Yeshua
2. High Priest
3. Yeshua

Shipwrecked!
1. Bad weather
2. Malta
3. Viper (snake)

Priscilla & Aquila
1. Tent-makers
2. Claudius ordered all Jews to leave Rome
3. Corinth

Tabitha, Arise!
1. She became ill
2. Two men
3. She opened her eyes and sat up

Philip & the Ethiopian
1. An Ethiopian eunuch
2. Isaiah the prophet
3. Yeshua the Messiah

Timothy
1. Lystra
2. Greek
3. Phrygia and Galatia

Mary & Martha
1. Bethany
2. Mary
3. Spikenard

Zacchaeus
1. Tax collector
2. Because he was short and couldn't see Yeshua
3. Half of his goods

✧◇ DISCOVER MORE ACTIVITY BOOKS! ◇✧

Available for purchase at www.biblepathwayadventures.com

INSTANT DOWNLOAD!

100 Bible Quizzes   Bereshit / Genesis
The Fall Feasts   Moses Ten Plagues
Bible Heroes   Birth of The King
Women of the Bible   Bible Miracles

Made in the
USA
Columbia, SC